A HIGHER PURPOSE:
The Moral Equivalent of War

*Decoding America's Preamble
to Solve Our Leadership Crisis*

Richard D. Cheshire Ph.D.

Published by Hamilton House Publications, LLC
PO Box 89, Hamilton, New York 13346

Copyright 2018 by Richard D. Cheshire, Ph.D.

ISBN-13-978-1975643751

ISBN 10:1975643755

BISAC: Political Science/General

TABLE OF CONTENTS

Dedicated to Our Founding Fathers

These innovators, given the times and circumstances that they lived in, created a new nation that could and would build upon their insights, the prescience and the promises they made to become the leading nation in the free world. They launched this new nation with the following words, known as the Preamble to the United States Constitution:

We the People of the United States, in Order to form a more perfect Union, establish Justice, insure domestic Tranquility, provide for the common defence, promote the general Welfare, and secure the Blessings of Liberty to ourselves and our Posterity, do ordain and establish this Constitution for the United States of America.

FOREWORD

Many years have gone by since Dick Cheshire and I graduated from Colgate University in Hamilton, New York. To chronicle the changes that have happened, the views that have emerged, and the challenges that have occurred would take up a lot of memory that is in the cloud. I was fortunate enough to renew my friendship and association with Dick after I moved back to Hamilton to pursue the creation of a model intergenerational community nearby his retirement home well over a decade ago.

Since then he and I have looked at the paths we have followed, the education we have gained, and the proposals for solutions we'd like to share. He rediscovered the Preamble to the Constitution as the guide star to once again bring "We the People of the United States" back together as envisioned and promised in 1787.

I joined him in creating the Promise America Alliance to analyze, gather, and organize partners to remember the leadership of the Preamble that could empower the nation again as our guide to promoting national unity.

We believe that in addition to raising public awareness, and persuading leaders to incorporate these values and promises into their priorities, that annual reports on national progress available to the public, pundits and politicians need to be created and disseminated. We have, therefore, been doing the data analysis that is planned for an upcoming Promise America Report or PAR measuring tool, as we imagine it.

As a lifelong golfer, I believe that setting a standard of excellence, as in par, and seeing if we are measuring up to it—aiming at achieving par or even exceeding it—is our basic challenge. Steve Ballmer's recent work has launched his *usa.facts* project that collects data related to the Preamble that can provide a great source of initial information.

This is the way the Founders of this nation saw how it would grow, be creative, and prosper. What directions to be pursued would emanate from "We the People" who would be creating "a more perfect Union", focusing on certain basic principles in order to "secure the Blessings of Liberty to ourselves and our Posterity."

This is a time for opportunity, for agreeing on basic principles and then having a proper and realistic discussion of how best to realize them given our time and place, keeping in mind that we are looking at ourselves as one people, the driving force that can, indeed, work to achieve "a more perfect Union."

Arthur William Rashap, J.D., LL.M., Editor,
Co-Chair of the Promise America Alliance.
Charlottesville, Virginia 2018

INTRODUCTION

A PREAMBLE OF HIGHER PURPOSE

The politically polarized government of the United States has led to an erosion of American leadership at home and in the world. This is something we do not have to accept. It is something we can fix. We've overcome adversity before—particularly in wars we've won, and more recently lost. What we need now to embrace is the "moral equivalent of war,"[1] touted more than a century ago by William James, the leading scholar of American pragmatism, that brings us to a system of national leadership that is energized by a sharp clarity of high purpose—the core rationale of our mission, strategy and leadership—about which we are historically and functually illiterate.

Our Founding Fathers, led by James Madison of Virginia, set forth America's national purpose in the Preamble of the United States Constitution. To

Americans there are no more important words which tell us who we want to be.

This is our core rationale as a nation, yet we are shockingly oblivious to what this first Constitutional sentence says, not to mention what it means. Without a common understanding of our purpose as a nation, we are in forbidding trouble amid a world of stress that needs our unselfish leadership. This lack of worldly purpose prevents us from concentrating on pragmatic solutions to address our most pressing problems. Shared clarity of purpose is essential for leadership in any organizational system. And the lack of higher purpose is deadly for leadership in a globalized system.

The United States is an open society with an organized system. The working purpose of any organized system has to keep simultaneously in mind its electrodynamics, its genetic code, and its leadership ethic in order for it to work. This is not hard to understand if we are clearheaded about it.

In the first place, its electrodynamics or nervous system must facilitate an impetus of creative leadership which is strong enough to convert the actions of individual people into the momentum of a unified body of supporters that can move in a common direction at a standard velocity according to its impetus-action-momentum dynamics written as $I=am^2$. This is the equation of leadership we are introducing for that purpose. In short, it stands for "We" instead of "Me."

In the second place, the formative genetic code or DNA of creative energy drives (D) its collaborators into a center of gravity that forms a nucleus (N) as a critical mass of associated people who, in turn, reach a tipping point from which they accelerate (A) in a chain reaction, thus fulfilling the intended high purpose of its body politic or ODNA, that is, its organizational DNA.

In the third place, a momentum of high purpose creates a group of collaborating leaders who exemplify an ancient leadership practice turned into a new and more powerful leadership ethic. This ethic embodies the greatest possible good, for the largest number of people, over the longest period of time, at the lowest necessary cost to serve their high purpose or core rationale.

With such a purpose, these three networked data points—the $I=am^2$ architecture, the ODNA accelerator, and the new leadership ethic—must work simultaneously to implement the ideals of the Preamble. The United States has grown and developed as a creative experiment in republican democracy. In America all citizens are connected by their common "stream of life", as George Washington called it, or America's DNA as it may be called today. And our historic reputation as a land of opportunity and diversity has welcomed immigrants such as Alexander Hamilton, Albert Einstein and Sergey Brin of Google among many others who have helped make America the nation of immigrants it is today and has been since its birth.

As we travel down this purpose-driven networked pathway, we can more readily turn our angry argumentation into civilized debate and more surely re-establish American leadership in the world. To do that well, as my partner Arthur Rashap has noted, we will need to create an objective, nonpartisan measure as an annual accounting of the national condition—we'll call it the *Promise America Report* or simply *PAR*—from which we may realize a most hopeful future.

America's leadership among nations arises less from military and economic power alone, but from something much greater when combined with political power. The firepower of military might and the financial power of economic growth are powerful, but far stronger when bolstered by the political power of human hearts and minds. This is particularly so when devoted to a compelling cause, or sense of high purpose, such as "liberty and justice for all" as in our Pledge of Allegiance. In such a case, leadership will have reached a sustainable leading status no matter what occurs otherwise. The creative energy present in this circumstance produces a center of gravity strong enough to form a critical mass of military, economic, and political power. This power can then reach a tipping point that triggers a continuous chain reaction as long as these three conditions prevail, as we believe the Promise America Reports will help demonstrate..

For the creative connections of America's political, economic and military power to be turned on simultaneously we must rewire our system of organized government into the digital equivalent of the human nervous system, that is, an integrated system of non-classified information transfer, or "digital nervous system," as Bill Gates has called it.[2] This plugs us more fully into human nature from which our civility is derived. The spirit of the law which governs us as a nation is then activated, person by person, leader by leader. The evolution of all forms of association take their form and function accordingly.

Every American embodies a part of the future as a whole. We are independent human beings created by our interdependence with others. Our interdependence is the pillar on which we create our families, our communities, our associations of all kinds, including our nation as a whole. Simply put: "I am" becomes "we are." Our creativity is fundamental not only to our existence but to our well-being. This leads to Albert Einstein's "equation of equations."

That is the famous $E=mc^2$ universal equation of creativity in which energy equals mass times the speed of light squared. According to this long verified formula, everything in our world is creative energy of one form or another. That includes us. We are not things. We are human beings: body, mind and soul. Einstein's formula set in motion what came to be called the *theory of relativity*. What hasn't been developed is a counterpart that applies specifically to human beings, that is, a *theory of relationship* compatible with this universal equation of creativity. We humans interact self-consciously with an experienced sense of our environment. How do we do that? Why does it matter?

The relationship counterpart that we may postulate is written as $I=am^2$—impetus equals action times momentum squared. The impetus of leadership equals the actions of individual people turned into the momentum of a unified group. Before *I am,* there is the movement that is framed according to $I=am^2$. The independence of one person starts with the interdependence of two persons through the nurturing of mothers and fathers. Yes, "we are."

This has a fundamental relation to the success of families, businesses, and nations. The simple idea is that two originates one so that one may originate more. What each one of us goes on to do as a person connects with others one way or another, from the Garden of Eden to the Promised Land, to whatever we make of our circumstances. This is where leadership as we know it makes its appearance. Organized groups form around particular interests. People lead themselves and are led by others. Where? To what end?

$I=am^2$ is the measuring tool of some higher purpose—expressing the moral equivalent of war—that initiates and supports a system of leadership. One leads to many. We cherish our independence and self reliance as well as our connections with each other. We are independent persons and, even more importantly, interdependent people. The impetus of leadership by one or more people is the equivalent of the action of others who follow, multiplied by the square of the momentum they generate together. $I=am^2$. This is the human relationship equivalent of Einstein's $E=mc^2$ formula of creativity which is the first step toward our higher purpose, that begins with this leading equation.

This—the moral equivalent of war— is what we will explore here. We will do this using the $I=am^2$ equation of leadership that wires us together with our world. What will we make of it? That is the

American challenge we will address. The launching pad will be the first sentence of the Constitution which we know as the Preamble. Its first word let us remember, is "We."

PART ONE

OUR MISSION–THE INPUT

CHAPTER 1

WE THE PEOPLE OF THE UNITED STATES

"We the People of the United States" are the inheritors of the founding ideals of America as they were authored by our Founding Fathers in the United States Constitution. This nation, and those other nations which have followed or borrowed from America's leadership, have fostered the principles of creativity and growth through a myriad of major initiatives over the years. The ideals and principles are reflected in the leading words of the Preamble.

"We the People of the United States, in Order to form a more perfect Union, establish Justice, insure domestic Tranquility, provide for the common defence, promote the general Welfare, and secure the Blessings of Liberty to ourselves

and our Posterity, do ordain and establish this Constitution for the United States of America."

These words set forth the national purpose of the United States. They represent the philosophy of the Founding Fathers who, without dissent, introduced them in 1787. These principles were grounded in the leading work of Enlightenment thinkers in Europe from whom all of the Founding Fathers' ancestors had come. These principles were later applied and transformed by leading philosophers in America who invented pragmatism and advocated it on the world stage in the late 19th and early 20th century. Now, as we make our way into the middle of the 21st century, we are accountable in our role as a major world leader for overcoming a polarized and under-performing reality. The great challenge for America today, at home and abroad, is to keep these founding principles alive, to remember them for our age and times, and above all, for the future.

The intention here is to relate the processes of leadership to operate through a concerned and concerted body of individuals by their shared DNAs, and through organizations with their ODNAs, that can create major changes. There is also a deeply needed process to be implemented regarding what impetus or driving force can bring "We the People" together utilizing the principles and promises the founders foresaw as the path to well-being of the people and our world.

As we will see, there is the impetus (I) of creative energy in a free and fair country that is supported and protected by a limited government which develops centers of gravity to generate a critical mass for more productive action (a). This then reaches a tipping point that converts this productive action into chain reactions of momentum (m^2) for prosperity and well-being while, at all times, moving at the universal speed of light. $I=am^2$ is an architecture of leadership that can hold together our higher purpose. This is the "We" of any leadership anywhere, anytime.

In the lead-up to ratification of the new Constitution, there was an unnoticed coincidence which helped anticipate the creativity that has driven America's leadership since the birth of the nation. Alexander Hamilton emphasized national "energy" as the crux of a strong federal government. George Washington wrote of a unified "mass" of the means and efforts of different people. Ben Franklin's famous kite and key experiment demonstrated the connection between "light" and electricity.

These Founding Fathers were among the 55 delegates sent by their states to consider how to bring the new nation more effectively together to solve the problems faced under the Articles of Confederation. They were present at the Constitutional Convention in Philadelphia in 1787. They and their colleagues gave their collective voice to the greatest promise ever made to those in the new nation and to the generations that followed. This promise was set forth in the ten phrases of the fifty-two word Preamble of the U. S. Constitution which state our national purpose, our highest ideals, and our working standards. This promise, however, has been essentially ignored in American politics despite the fact that government leaders are all sworn to support and defend the Constitution as their oath of office.

Although the thoughts of Hamilton about energy, Washington about mass, and Franklin about light happened serendipitously, they anticipated Albert Einstein's universal law of creativity that came more than a century later. This law forms the architecture of all leadership. It describes a set of invariant energy, mass, and light relationships which came to be called the *theory of relativity* and is well known for its $E=mc^2$ formula. This universal law, in retrospect, underlies the creativity, through darkness and light, by which America found the prosperity set in motion years ago by the Founding Fathers.

These relationships of the universal law of creativity were very much in play during the give and take in 1787 Philadelphia during the Constitutional Convention. While Einstein, coming much later, had nothing to do with the Founders, he explicitly formulated the basis of what they had incorporated into the launching of this great experiment called the United States of America. They had produced a foundation for a free and creative nation. Einstein was not only the author of the formula for the natural law of creativity, but a great scientist and humanitarian who, later in life, left his native Germany and its Nazi leaders for America and the Institute for Advanced Studies at Princeton, in New Jersey, and who subsequently became a naturalized American citizen.

Now, it is necessary to consider what we will refer to as a *theory of relationship* by which energy, mass and light lead to interconnections of micro-interpersonal relations with macro-international affairs. These human relationships correspond with the *theory of relativity* and its leading equation of $E=mc^2$.

$E=mc^2$ frames what Einstein called "the electrodynamics of moving bodies" as in the human DNA and its ODNA organizational counterpart. They may be converted, in essence, to the psychodynamics of human beings in the $I=am^2$ equation in which the impetus of leadership is the equivalent of action by individual persons transformed into the momentum of a unified group of people. This transformation of $E=mc^2$ into $I=am^2$ makes a great deal of difference when we look at the conduct of human affairs as participation in creative processes, whether they work for good or ill.

This impetus equates to the "energy" about which Hamilton wrote. This action is the "mass" of which Washington spoke. And this momentum is the "light" which Franklin found.

The *theory of relationship* is of utmost importance today. It is the prospective framework for a dialogue that could deter the destruction of America's moral authority. Losing this moral authority is turning an American political crisis into a world leadership crisis. The fundamental asset of America's leadership is the moral foundation of freedom and democracy that is rooted in the Preamble. If America fails to refocus its governing dynamics back to their foundation in the Preamble, it could lead to disastrous consequences both domestically and with the rest of the world.

To keep the promise America made, "We the People" must see that it does.

CHAPTER 2

TO FORM A MORE PERFECT UNION

The reality or unreality of America as leader of the free world—a complex, debatable, and influential idea—can now be more clearly understood with the assistance of the leading equation—$I=am^2$, declaring who *"we are,"* from one to more and from more to one—to form the ties that bind, and in so doing, generate the *Impetus* of leadership that converts the *action* of individuals into the *momentum* of a unified group. This is the core of human creativity that has long been at the heart of our democratic republic. Because that equation is an application of Einstein's epic $E=mc^2$ "equation of all equations", it is there to be applied to human relationship issues of every conceivable nature. $I=am^2$ is human nature's equivalent of Mother Nature's $E=mc^2$— "in Order to form a more perfect Union."

Thomas Jefferson's July 4, 1776 Declaration of Independence begins:

"When in the Course of human events, it becomes necessary for one people to dissolve the political bonds which have connected them with another, and to assume among the powers of the earth, the separate and equal station to which the Laws of Nature and Nature's God entitle them, a decent respect for the opinions of mankind requires that they should declare the causes which impel them to the separation."

Now, Einstein's work has led to a rethinking of our world as part of a dynamic universe of creative possibilities instead of the mechanistic "clockwork universe" that had dominated scientific thought for centuries. His work, in turn, has led to ongoing technological advances of an increasingly industrialized and globalized world. $E=mc^2$ is now recognized as the universal law of creativity, from nuclear medicine to the atomic bomb and beyond, the critical algorithm of the universe.

The implications of this universal equation, and the general theory that followed, traced the impulse of creativity to its origin and then to its vast implications for research and technology that followed in America and the world. What it did not do was to connect material creativity with the human creativity that discovered and explained it in the first place.

What, then, would become of $E=mc^2$'s derivative for creative human relationships which is $I=am^2$, that is, the *Impetus* of leadership that equals the variety of *action* among independent people as individuals times the *momentum* of interdependent people as a unified group. Leading to one, a unity of leaders and followers, is what leadership is about. $I=am^2$ is an equation which formulates the general rule of leadership at work among people.

Leadership organizes the potential of energy-at-rest into the kinetic actuality of energy-in-motion. In so doing, it produces a circle of influence that is the most creative force in every sphere of human activity. Its guiding brain circuit is, in essence, a metaphorical leader chip that emits nerve impulses analogous to a computer's microprocessor. All the elements of leading are present and functioning, in one manner or another. $I=am^2$ electromagnetically amplifies the messaging to and from the brain through the rest of the human nervous system.

These $I=am^2$ factors are the unseen lifestream of human relationships that correspond with the creative formula of the universe. In 1637, Rene Descartes opined that: "I think, therefore I am." He reasoned that if I can think, I am recognizing my status as a person. This simple thought became a profound step of reasoning toward the emergence of modern thought that led to the sweeping impact of the Enlightenment from across Europe to political leaders in America. Coincidentally the liberating possibilities of $I=am^2$ began to shape the thoughts of liberty and equality that captivated our Founding Fathers.

These thoughts could be traced back to the old biblical story of freedom in the Book of Exodus. Whether or not Einstein was familiar with this pillar of scripture, he was a believer in "The Old One"[3], his preferred name for God. Our founding leaders were determined to declare and enact our independence from King George and his autocratic Parliament. And the idea of freedom could be seen as a God-given gift of "The Old One" deep in the consciences of the founders, whatever their religious beliefs were.

The Exodus story in scripture tells of the shepherd Moses encountering a burning bush on Mount Sinai from which an authoritative voice he thought to be that of Yahweh, the God of the Israelites, commanded him to tell the Pharaoh "let my people go", referring to Moses' Israelites who were enslaved by the Egyptian king. When Moses asked who shall I say sent me, the voice replied "I AM

WHO I AM...I AM is my name forever...I will be with you and will lead the Israelites...to a land flowing with milk and honey" that was the promised land from the Israelite's God Yahweh as a gift to their father Abraham and his ancestors.

To the Israelites as children of God, the words understood by Moses meant "I was, I am, and I will be." The past, present and future were wrapped up in the eternal. I AM would lead them to the land of milk and honey. Exodus meant liberation. Taking together the freedom of Exodus and the creativity of Einstein, $I=am^2$ may be used as an algorithm—the basis of calculations for action and creation in the universe and the code of our more or less purposeful human relationships. Einstein was neither a practicing Jew nor an atheist. Rather, he was often known to consider his pursuits as learning what "The Old One" had in mind for the universe, and for him.

From the omnipresence of "The Old One" and the pervasiveness of creative energy in all of nature raises the question of whether God and energy co-exist in some form of unified relationship, ultimately acting as one, such as "in God is the creative energy," or "in the creative energy is God." Thus, "The Old One" would presumably be the Creator, although Einstein never claimed that. If so, that could help clarify how the right and left brains work as one brain in human beings. "The Old One," then, would be the primal source of both their unity and their diversity as children of God.

Leadership in all things and among everyone would consist of a powerful creative energy that, through persuasion, turns independent individuals into sources of influence comprised of interdependent people. If the pull of that influence is strong enough, it develops into a critical mass that reaches a tipping point of change. When that occurs there is a transition like that of turning water into ice or into steam. The pull of a growing mass then overtakes the status quo and initiates a chain reaction that, if strong enough, reaches an output sufficient to support the sustenance of an ongoing mass. This chain reaction realizes the change which leadership has sought in the first place. This is as true for human beings as it is for living water or rising steam.

But, what about in the first place? Going back to the emergence of our universe following the "Big Bang," Einstein imagined "The Old One," and declared that "a spirit is manifest in the laws of the universe—a spirit vastly superior to that of man and one in the face of which we, with our modest powers must feel humble."[4] Subsequently, Stephen Hawking posed a question: "Why is there something rather than nothing?" And he then speculated: "If we find the answer to that, it would be the ultimate triumph of human reason—for then we should know the mind of God."[5]

But, how would our understanding of the mind of God work? By faith and reason, religion and science? Yes, if we see them as two avenues to the same unified destination—a universe of creative energy coincident with God as Father and Mother of us all. That seems to be the way Einstein saw it. All through his professional life he sought a unified field theory, yet he did not find it. Meantime, physicists across the world have built a standard model to supply an architecture for the workings of the universe. In 2012 team leaders at the Large Hadron Collider near Geneva, Switzerland, where the research was concentrated, announced that they had found the Higgs Boson, the context of a mass-creating energy field that wraps around and penetrates the universe. The cosmic particles passing through this energy field took on various configurations of mass that eventually shaped the Earth and everything on it.

The Higgs Boson was dubbed the "God Particle" by Nobel laureate Leon Lederman for its ubiquitous creativity.[5] Those who believed in God didn't like it because it didn't fit well with their spirituality. Those who didn't believe in God also didn't like it because it didn't fit well with their idea of the universe. But it proved to have great box office appeal and headline news following among those who became curious to learn more about it.

Leadership originates from the oneness of our universe and the creative energy field that integrates and develops the world as we know it. This oneness, we may believe, comes from the God of Abraham who is recognized by the followers of Judaism, Christianity, and Islam as the Father-and-Mother of their divine faiths. This God has been known by Jews as Yahweh whose prophet is Moses. Christians recognize God by this name whose son is Jesus, their Messiah. This same God is known as Allah by Muslims whose prophet is Muhammad. Apart from God, many believe, there is nothingness.

In the digital world could this be God [1], and nothingness [0]. Do the two interact to create the future? Gottfried von Leibniz argued, as David Berlinski tells the story, that "there are only two absolutely simple concepts, God and Nothingness. From these," Leibniz further postulated that: "all other concepts may be constructed, the world and everything in it." That led him to realize that "what is crucial . . . is the *alternation* between God and nothingness. And for this," he said, "the numbers 0 and 1 suffice."[7] This, it could be contended, eventually led to computer programming calculations that helped set in motion the digital revolution we are experiencing today.

The three divine religions demand social justice for everyone as their rule for all. In their different ways they see God as both Creator of the universe and redeemer for those who follow him. Today these faiths comprise more than half the world's people and growing. Their leadership teaches that compassion, humility, and freedom are needed to find the truth about one's higher calling in a world at peace.

In America, members of Congress, the President, and Supreme Court justices all take an oath of office to abide by—that is, support, protect, and defend—the Constitution of the United States. The

Constitution is led by a Preamble that lays the foundation for the new nation's future. When considered with the scripture of the three divine faiths, one can see the essentials of "The Golden Rule" which may be stated as: "do unto others as you would have them do unto you." And the pledge of allegiance to the flag declares "one nation under God, with liberty and justice for all."

To keep the promise America made, we must "form a more perfect Union."

PART TWO

OUR STRATEGY-
THE THROUGHPUT

CHAPTER 3

ESTABLISH JUSTICE

As the Constitution's draftsmen seem to have seen it, to "establish Justice" is, in effect, step one of what would be America's grand strategy—that began with enabling the productivity necessary to overcome the new nation's threatening difficulties in meeting the financial underpinnings of equality. Justice requires the ability to do what is right and proper for the greater good, whatever that may be, no matter who might be involved. In a just society, people are treated with respect. Relationships are sustained by mutuality and trust. "Equal Justice Under Law," emblazoned on the facade of the United States Supreme Court building in Washington D.C., reminds us of our shared humanity and sacred duty.

"The moral arc of the universe is long," Martin Luther King, Jr. proclaimed, "but it bends toward justice." Does it? The major religions of the world share a commitment to justice as a necessary component that enables people to live together. Albert Einstein declared his belief that "Subtle is the Lord, but malicious he is not." King was a preacher and moral philosopher. Einstein was a scientist and worldly philosopher. Both were persecuted because of their corresponding views about creativity and leadership.

King was right that "you don't have to know Einstein's relativity theory to serve." But it was Einstein who produced the relativity theory and its famous $E=mc^2$ algorithm, which later became the icon of modern science and technology. He was also a spiritual and humanitarian person, though he never applied his famous algorithm to humanity itself even though it "sums up all action and creation in the universe,"[8] according to the words of one of his biographers.

We are now called to apply the law of Mother Nature to human nature with the $I=am^2$ proposition that "we are." We do not need to change Einstein's ultimate algorithm, but simply apply its mandate to everyday life. Body and mind act as one. Truth matters. Interdependence is truth. $I=am^2$ implements that. The Impetus of leadership, wherever it begins, continues as the actions (and reactions) of individual people generate change (or do not) that builds momentum (or does not). Scripture and schooling teach that "the truth shall make you free." Justice requires support for this freedom, or we are in danger of losing it.

Thus, we must "establish justice," that is, equal opportunity, equal protection, and fair treatment of everyone in all civic circumstances as the Preamble directs us. This, then, sets forth the first step of a grand strategy to implement the American mission for "We the People of the United States, in Order to form a more perfect Union."

For humanity among all, we must have justice for all. When we have justice, it leads to tranquility. The solidarity that follows tranquility supports the common defense. Once safety from attack is achieved, it opens a path to general welfare. Thus, the national mission is enabled by a grand strategy of justice, tranquility, defense and welfare to help the nation become more productive for, by and of the people.

It was envisioned that ours would be an open society functioning within an organized system. In such a system there is a dynamic set of interconnected parts where the so-called "butterfly effect" can produce large effects from small changes. As Margaret Mead said "Never doubt that a small group of thoughtful committed citizens can change the world; indeed, it's the only thing that ever has."[9] The butterfly effect produces ongoing uncertainty in dynamic systems, which a healthy democracy is. It often works through unexpected and even hidden drivers that overcome current conditions.

Our future as a free country is founded on the principles written in the Preamble to the

Constitution—elaborated in the Bill of Rights, and further specified in subsequent amendments—that are derived from nature's laws. More specifically, they are the basis of human nature. Without justice—primarily equality before the law—there would be no human nature. All nature would be sub-human. Humanity could not have risen because the self-centeredness of people would have led to their extinction. As Archbishop Desmond Tutu exclaimed: "Because we need one another, our natural tendency is to be cooperative and helpful. If this were not true we would have died out as a species long ago, consumed by our violence and hate."[10]

In a talk on leadership with a group of high school honor society members years ago I asked them how they would spell it. They got it right, of course, but I told them "no", they had it wrong. It is better spelled e-m-p-o-w-e-r-m-e-n-t, I suggested. Because, at its best, leadership transforms prospective followers into dedicated followers, non-leaders into co-leaders, empowered to be partners who actively share in the general leadership. Equal opportunity participation would take the place of less powerful precast roles.

The Preamble sets the table for a just society with principles that enable Americans to prosper together. All principles serve a purpose based in the legitimacy of a mission, as in "We the People of the United States, in Order to form a more perfect Union." The legitimacy is from the people. The mission is for a more perfect union of the people in the nation.

Establishing justice requires a humanity that leads to civic virtue. And civic virtue comes from the expectations of "life, liberty, and the pursuit of happiness."[11] Each of the divine religions— Judaism, Christianity, and Islam—lifts up justice as the heart of their faith. Civilization and faith are, therefore, joined together as two sides of the same story.

Abraham Lincoln memorably observed:

"Our reliance is in our love for liberty; our defense is in the spirit which prizes liberty as the heritage of all people in all lands everywhere. Destroy this spirit, and we have planted the seeds of despotism at our own doors. Those who deny freedom to others do not deserve it for themselves, and cannot long retain it. Why should there not be a patient confidence in the ultimate justice of the people? Is there any better or equal hope in the world? Let us have faith that right makes might, and in that faith, let us, to the end, dare to do our duty as we understand it."[12]

We urgently need, therefore, to rediscover and remember these founding principles and the nature of the nation foreseen by the founders of these United States of America who produced them. This would enable our current leaders to more readily and steadily do their jobs for all Americans and the world. This would engage our fellow citizens today with the principles our founders set forth yesterday. And it would provide a clearer context for skilled leadership going forward.

America's leadership in a free world was established in the late 18th century by a congress of such distinguished leaders as never had been seen before. They created the first written constitution in world history. They created the makings of a democracy when all other nations were ruled by autocratic governments. They introduced their draft of a national Constitution with a set of principles called the Preamble to guide interpretations of the nine articles, as well as the 27 amendments which followed later.

What would the words of the Preamble mean for keeping these founding principles alive as a working reference for now? In terms of our thinking today, the words of the Preamble speak directly to America's **mission** as a nation—*"We the people of the United States, in order to form a more perfect union"*—to our **strategy** for realizing that mission—*"establish justice, insure domestic* *tranquility, provide for the common defense, promote the general welfare'*—and the **leadership** necessary to implement that strategy in order to create momentum for the mission—*"and secure the blessings of liberty, to ourselves and our posterity, do ordain and establish this Constitution for the United States of America."*

To start with, America's momentum today is flagging. Since the Second World War, it has clearly been the leader of a free world. Today, there are uncertainties about the direction of our leadership and instabilities in our government in Washington and around the nation. Despite the strength of our economy and military, our politics has slowed our momentum as global leader. Yet we are still the world's most powerful nation, conflicts notwithstanding.

Momentum can be sustainable, but is not automatic. At its core, the Impetus of leadership is sustained by converting the actions of citizens into the momentum of their unity as a respected nation.

Without unity, citizenship is weakened. Its absence makes effective leadership far more difficult and less likely.

Leadership requires followers. Shared principles are ties that bind. Civic virtue is essential. Good sound education and responsible, accessible voting are a necessity. Enlightenment, pragmatism, and accountability are all at the nucleus of leadership. In a democratic republic such as ours, both leadership and followership are worthy of the greatest attention and respect.

Enlightened leadership is a spiritual act. Whatever its nature, it emanates from the soul. Pragmatic leadership is a matter of shared vision, faith, and accountability. Such leadership can be deeply felt, and capable of releasing significant energy that leads to action and momentum.

There actually is, as noted, aside from popular assumptions, an unrecognized leadership algorithm that connects high imagination with on-the-ground practicality and that jointly contributes to advancement of any purpose in any situation. This algorithm emerges from sources in science and religion. As Einstein observed: "Science without religion is lame, religion without science is blind."[13]

The implications of this equation, and the theory that followed, traced the universal impulse of creativity to its origin and then to its vast implications for research and technology that followed in America and the world. What it did not do was to connect material creativity with the human creativity that discovered and explained it. Though Einstein was a great humanitarian, his scientific focus was fundamental physics, not synchronized civics.

$I=am^2$ is driven by its purpose, our equation of leadership, and how it serves our pragmatic philosophy. We can imagine it as the flip side of Einstein's famous $E=mc^2$ equation of creativity (or destruction). It can begin with the words of one and be multiplied by the thoughts of many. The Impetus of leadership converts the action of one or more leading individuals into the momentum of a unified and growing group, however great or small. We cannot even imagine something nor do something until we first have an image of it in our minds, which is surely why Einstein said: "Imagination is more important than knowledge." Images come before our capacity to verbalize or name what we see.

The potential of impetus depends upon the intensity of experience. This intensity works not only vertically and more formally through family trees and other hierarchies. It also works horizontally and more informally through extended families and other associations. It may be developed through friends and acquaintances at work. It may be encountered and acquired at home, in neighborhoods and schools, or at church and in other social settings.

In all cases, these relationships are shaped pragmatically by what works for those who are involved, the working participants. Leadership grows through the magnets of individual attention and attraction, to the appeal and acceptance of groups. The stronger the relationship the more powerful the influence. The greater the influence the more powerful the persuasion. Leading relationships are, more particularly, about moral suasion, not about the command and control which is at the core of management. Leading relationships are about collaboration and consent in which the impetus of leadership transforms the various actions of people as independent agents into the momentum of people as part of an interdependant group.

Management and leadership are partners, with clearly important differences. Management is more often a commanding relationship. Leadership is more often a collaborative relationship. The more complicated a particular task may be, the more likely it is a mix of both. Flexibility is a necessity. I=am^2 applies differently to leadership and management.

I=am^2 is most accountable when it examines the nature of relationships. If, for example, we are considering the Constitution, where do we start? Its beginning is the Preamble, the first words of the law of the land. Articles 1, 2, and 3 are about the Congress, the President, and the Supreme Court which follow. The first ten amendments we know as the Bill of Rights, particularly the first which addresses the rights of the people to the establishment and exercise of religion, freedom of speech and the press, peaceable assembly, and redress of grievances. The second amendment speaks to the right of the people to keep and bear arms.

With a closer look, whatever one's politics, we find a constitutional architecture for leadership that is well grounded^2 to protect the country from autocracy, but less so to promote it for democracy. In fact, this truth has created a structure that is essentially unsusceptible to anything less than the appropriately skillful leadership for a diverse population such as we are and always have been. This structure was severely tested by secession and civil war, and is now being tested from many directions such as elections and voting, legislative rules and executive actions, judicial decisions and access to review. This would be a task most difficult for any President, not to mention any Congress or Court, who are charged with forging a current and future direction for the public at large. Political polarization has only made such issues virtually impossible to resolve without a leadership process that does not yet exist.

The leader's way is the first and foremost task of the President. Yet, in our democracy the leader's way applies to everyone. The President cannot and should not be expected to do this alone. Leadership requires a core purpose and a clear message that more or less drives the dynamics of people in government and throughout the country. And that core message is based on the principles articulated in the Preamble. They are the constant requirements of a more or less receptive constituency. Whatever the message may be, it must be consistently updated based on the latest information and intelligence regarding the greatest concerns.

With the advent of high technology, virtually all information leads to decision-making that demands faster and smarter responses in order to effectively address truth from falsehood at home and abroad—that is how the information is organized, analyzed, and presented so that decisions may be made properly and effectively. How does $I=am^2$ help us do that?

Think of $I=am^2$ as the framework of a learning system about who we are: an integrated circuit connected to a conscious mind and a functional nervous system. This integrated circuit would be analogous to a computer's microprocessor that serves as a metaphorical leader chip. To take best advantage of this, think of $I=am^2$ as our leader chip. The leader chip amplifies the messaging to and from the brain and the nervous system. The wiring of the connecting points in the $I=am^2$ equation activates and sustains a network of leadership.

In 2005, the New York Times ran a 100th anniversary op-ed by Brian Greene, the distinguished scientist and best-selling author at Columbia University, who extolled Einstein's famous formula in these words:

There is nothing you can do, not a move you can make, not a thought you can have, that doesn't tap directly into $E=mc^2$. Einstein's equation is constantly at work, providing an unseen hand that shapes the world into its familiar form.[14]

This is a clear statement about the universal impact of creativity as Einstein discovered it.

To keep the promise America made, we must "establish Justice."

CHAPTER 4

INSURE DOMESTIC TRANQUILITY

Science historian Timothy Ferris has written that "The Golden Rule is invariant across the human species and hence is widely regarded as an objective basis for ethics generally."[15] Where people treat each other with respect, even in trying circumstances, there is a deep belief that it is both principled and practical to "do unto others as you would have them do to you," or we might say, "to anyone" as the history of world religions would allow us to add.

This belief is fundamental to our new leadership ethic which is too often unobserved and therefore unpracticed. For our system of leadership to work, there must be a mutual dedication among those engaged to achieve a higher purpose toward which their effort is intended. This needs to be supported by a disciplined system of measurement, such as the PAR measurement tool, mentioned earlier, to keep them informed. To make a difference, there must be a shared measure of nonpartisan ownership in the higher purpose. Each participant has an acknowledged role or place in the greater scheme of things. Each has a purposeful mission. In regard to the purpose there is little or no room for differences once that purpose is established. Tranquility is, therefore, present in a state of mutual concentration. Teamwork.

This was very much on the founders minds as they began drafting the Preamble and the rest of the text for the proposed Constitution. James Madison of Virginia, "the father of the Constitution if there ever was one,"[16] according to historian Gordon Wood, was convinced by his experience as a member of the Virginia state legislature amid similar reports from elsewhere, that the primary problem was the "deficiencies of the state governments" whose self-serving ways were disabling the nation's ability to levy taxes, pay its debts, regulate commerce, and uphold its standing in international trade and foreign affairs.

The Shays Rebellion of 1786 in western Massachusetts was an uprising of some 4,000 armed rebels. There was concern and unrest over sharply fallen farm prices, heavy taxation that was apportioned unfairly, and a steep rise in land foreclosures. The participants were led by Captain Daniel Shays, a Revolutionary War veteran. As Henry Steele Commager reported, infuriated mobs disrupted court meetings and threatened the armory at Springfield after angry town meetings and an obstinate legislature that refused to enact necessary reforms: "The outbreak excited fear and despair in the hearts of many observers, and was not without influence in persuading Americans of the desirability of a stronger central government."[17]

No national government could long survive if preoccupied with such threats to its own internal security. Only a common sense of nonpartisan high purpose would produce the tranquility necessary to conduct the public business. If common sense justice prevailed, as the founders envisaged, it would lead to that necessary tranquility.

When Madison wrote in Federalist #10, he was increasingly concerned about domestic partisanship. "The instability, injustice, and confusion introduced into the public councils, have, in truth, been the mortal diseases under which popular governments have everywhere perished." He worried about "factions"—a term used for a united group of citizens who were passionately devoted to a special interest, even at the expense of the common interest. He knew that factions most often arose from the unfair and unequal distribution of property—either to protest the inequality or to take advantage of it. And he knew that in a republic education, voting, and legislation were main avenues to address it.[18]

This would require a well informed and organized public to correct unfair practices. Freedom of religion, speech, the press, and assembly—as in the First Amendment—would be essential to keep the public informed and engaged. And this would likely be a never ending priority of republican governments.

Domestic tranquility would, therefore, require the constant attention and timely regulation related to threats of inequality from the power and use of property. This, in turn, would necessitate transformative leadership as exemplified in the code of $I=am^2$.

The root of such leadership takes us back to the ancient, 6th century BCE, Chinese philosopher, Lao Tzu, author of the Tao Te Ching and founder of Taoism, which may be interpreted as the way of God. Lao Tzu is well known for his observation that:

A leader is best when people barely know that he exists, not so good when people obey and acclaim him, worst when they despise him. Fail to honor people, they fail to honor you. But of a good leader, who talks little when his work is done, his aims fulfilled, they will all say, 'We did it ourselves.'[19]

James MacGregor Burns' path breaking work has developed a generic formation for the consideration of transforming leadership, that is, leadership in its highest form and greatest power. Such leadership is what sustains tranquility because it meets the wants and needs of followers as they actively express them. This is critical because it generally removes the causes of dissension, anger and even violence. This is why "We the People" is so important as the introduction of the Constitution's Preamble. As Lincoln observed, this nation is of, by and for the people. Moral suasion is more likely to emerge where collaboration and consent are the norm. Moral suasion is part of human nature. Moral suasion is the most effective form of effective leadership. Moral suasion helps insure domestic tranquility.

The new leadership ethic—that is, the greatest possible good, for the largest number of people, over the longest period of time, at the lowest necessary cost—is fundamental to "insure domestic tranquility" because it rests upon the mutuality of respect by and for others. This reciprocity of conduct creates and supports the truth of partnership in all of human nature. Partners collaborate. Shared purpose drives their collaboration. Higher purpose elevates and excites the shared undertaking. Power is attached to moral authority—the good, the true, and the beautiful. The moral equivalent of war, and all its surrogates, recognizes the great and oft-unrealized strength of civility. And civility is the moral arc of the universe, however much it may struggle to be realized.

When people are treated with respect, they are happier than when they are not. When happy, they are friendly and calm, more likely to love than to fear. As FDR spoke in his first inaugural address in 1933: "the only thing we have to fear is fear itself—nameless, unreasoning, unjustified terror which paralyzes needed efforts to convert retreat into advance."[20] Fear and terror, whatever their source, are incendiary agitators leading to aggression. And aggression leads to war, in one form or another.

The founders were interested in staying out of war. So, they drew up the Constitution's Preamble as, in essence, the moral equivalent of war. The discipline and duty that accompanies armed conflict would be at the ready, but directed at negotiation of differences with necessary armaments in reserve in the event of a military threat. In actuality, the moral equivalent of war would be, for the new nation in its earliest years, a demanding struggle both domestically and internationally. The British and the French were at war. American shipping was being attacked. Overseas trade was suffering. There was no money for proper defense. The states were resistant to sharing tax income with the national government. When the Philadelphia convention came together in 1787, there was a clear and present danger of imminent national collapse.

Without domestic tranquility, there would be little hope for survival. James Madison, George Washington, Ben Franklin and their colleagues knew that, or at least suspected it, and were deeply concerned. This is why they approved the new Constitution, led by its Preamble, that would unify the American people in order to build the makings of a newly independent nation able to manage its own affairs. This is why they saw that the necessary responsibilities included what later came to be called the "moral equivalent of war." Thank you William James.

To keep the promise America made, we must "insure domestic Tranquility."

CHAPTER 5

PROVIDE FOR THE COMMON DEFENCE

The rock of ages is much more than an old hymn. It is a civic rock of energy, mass, and light which, at their foundations, are always in an unchanging relation to each other. Neither Hamilton, when he strove for energy in the executive, nor Washington when he cited the power of a mass of interests, nor Franklin when he discovered the electrical charge in the movement of light, would realize what the enormity of these separate phenomena would have when combined. And combined they are in an integrally related electrodynamics formula embedding all moving bodies in the universe.

More than a century after the launching of this new nation, it took Einstein, well before he became a naturalized American citizen in his later life, to realize the unity of the energy-mass-light relationship. It is only now, in the midst of deep disunity in the globalized world, that we see the implications of how the "electrodynamics of moving bodies" as Einstein put it, and the psychodynamics of human beings, as we are considering it, are all one, leading to the creative dynamics of a civil society. $I=am^2$ frames our destiny.

These dynamics convert creative energy through a center of gravity to a critical mass, then, via a tipping point, into a chain reaction moving at the speed of light through all aspects of our being. Their mutuality becomes a unity of relationship that blends into a solidarity of action and momentum. In their solidarity lies our security, their common defense against all threats from outside or inside our country. Ultimately and longer term, if not immediately and shorter term, security lies in the mass reaction of a unified nation which, as a civic rock, has put aside any more significant differences to concentrate on a clear and present urgency. This is true for a neighborhood, a nation, and the planet. This is the sequence or natural order of things until that natural order of things is obstructed or destructed. In times of national emergency, it is imperative to "provide for the common defence."

After the War of Independence had been won, the newborn nation created the Articles of Confederation to set forth the rules for government. However, the separate states were unable or unwilling to support an autonomous national government to protect themselves against harm from imminent foreign attack or immanent domestic violence, as in the Shays Rebellion.

Thanks primarily to the leadership of James Madison and George Washington, along with an evolving group of co-leaders, a convention of state delegates convened in Philadelphia. This became $I=am^2$ personified. And these delegates drafted the U.S. Constitution, now the oldest written constitution in the world. It is a constitution that has endured shameful compromise, dereliction of duty, and a horrendous civil war. It has endured because, in one case after another, the American people have ultimately and finally determined that there must be an outcome of union to all that transpires for the nation as a whole.

After World War II, the United States assumed significant responsibilities that enabled remarkable recoveries from widespread destruction in Europe and Japan. Fired by the emergence of a dynamic economy, U.S. leadership in the post-War world rose to superpower status backed by a strong military presence, a growing middle class economy, and new political confidence in the future.

What had been a wartime emergency buildup of weapons by manufacturing plants converted from domestic industry, segued into a post-war taxpayer-funded government-run defense industry which became known as the "military industrial complex," to use Dwight Eisenhower's term for it. The Korean War, Vietnam War, and the War in Iraq and Afghanistan, among other armed conflicts, required significant investment in the development of high technology weaponry—for land, sea and air capabilities—to deter the ongoing primary threat of the Soviet Union's Communist military expansion.

The United States military defense budgets have exceeded the Soviet's and eventually all other defense budgets across the world. The late 20th century collapse of the U.S.S.R. temporarily eased the pressure of the defense budget on all other U.S. budget priorities. However, it continues to dominate that of all other nations. Most recently, the urgencies of cyber security have rapidly risen as hostile activity, especially from Russia, threatens U.S. infrastructure networks essential to the functioning of the nation. Defense budgets have, therefore, continued to grow, domestic budgets have continued to suffer, and the national debt has continued to rise as budget deficits have ballooned.

The founders' definition of "the common defence" has rapidly expanded as the common defense became worldwide and significantly based on mutual security pacts, trade agreements, and military presence, however imperfectly structured or administered. Through all this, the prosperity and support of the American people has been the difference. But that is increasingly stretched as non-defense priorities have experienced budget shortages that threaten the well-being of more Americans whose livelihoods have not kept up with their requirements and expectations. Big changes with political risks are upon us. Does the Preamble shed any light on how to approach these changes and minimize the risks? Yes, it profoundly does. It is the introduction to law and order in our nation.

William James, the godfather of America's philosophy of pragmatism, gave a valedictory lecture at Stanford University in 1906 that spoke of a disciplined alternative to the ravages of war, and therefore defense. He saw it as the "moral equivalent of war" itself—with its casualties and bravery, commands and urgencies—in which a citizen would be required, when reaching a certain age, to enter into a general conscription for national service instead of just a specific conscription for military service. Though he did not address productivity explicitly, his focus supported the greater productivity of a nation at relative peace. In James's mind, civic service for national priorities would naturally and necessarily include military service as a standard option.[21]

George Washington observed that "to be prepared for war is one of the most effectual means of preserving peace." He also stressed that "the unity of government…is a main pillar in the edifice of your real independence, the support of your tranquility at home, your peace abroad, of your safety, of your prosperity, of that very liberty which you so highly prize."[22] National unity is national strength because it adds weight to the mass of a diverse people. That, of course, means the mass of citizens, one by one, must be enjoying a degree of happiness. And this, in turn, fosters an "attitude of gratitude," as is often said, and a willingness of citizens to sacrifice time and energy as civilian soldiers of the greater cause that defends the nation.

In a related manner, James considered the worthiness of each citizen as a contributing member of a civil society devoted to the pursuit of happiness—liberty and justice—for all. The implications of their contribution would "*promote the general welfare*"—in the words of the Constitution's Preamble—through more productive work. The net effect would reduce the need for corrective actions—regarding physical and mental health, compensatory education, unemployment and underemployment, incarceration and prison—that would tax public resources to a significantly greater extent. This would help ease the pressure on the nation's financial capability to hold true to its high purpose.

In such a milieu each person would embody the great Golden Rule of the world's major religions according to which we would "do unto others as we would have them do unto us." In James's world that would imagine pursuing the greater good rather than accepting an otherwise sicker society. This greater good would impact larger numbers of people in society over a longer period of time with fewer human resources expended. In essence, this new leadership ethic would supplant self before service with "service before self" as Rotary International, for one, actively supports across the world.

$I=am^2$ would be the facilitator of the common good, not just one's own interests. The code of purpose and leadership would provide a pathway to attract more opportunities, not a dead end. It would lay out a direction toward which more could be accomplished, especially for those who would need more help to be optimally productive.

Knowledge of $I=am^2$ as "we are" would help enable the development of high technology leadership in virtually every conceivable way. Computer programs, for example, are being designed and marketed for increasingly sophisticated learning about leadership in every imaginable pursuit—such as in health, education, and voting; in diplomacy, trade, and armaments; in R&D, manufacturing, and jobs; and in the sciences, the arts and the humanities.

The electromagnetic speed of light itself is a constant of all relationships in the non-visual micro world as well as in the commonly visual macro world. Thus, our vision is the product of our encompassing nervous system, including the brain, as seen through the lens of our eyes directed by the thoughts on our minds. The high technology of what we see and imagine mirrors the leading technology of our being itself. As a partner of Einstein's universal formula, the $I{=}am^2$ code of purpose is fundamental to all human relationships.

Our being is not limited to our individuality as persons. It includes our being part of all kinds of more or less organized associations. Just as individual persons have their own DNA, organized groups have their own organizational DNAs, or ODNAs. Think of DNA as being analogous to the lifestream of our $I{=}am^2$ model of creativity. DNA is short for deoxyribonucleic acid. Consider DNA metaphorically as the Driver (D), the Nucleus (N), and the Accelerator (A) of human relationships. It is applicable to our perceptions of individuals as well as of our organizations. ODNA is a notable basis, therefore, to serve as a core of leadership connected to our $I=am^2$ code of purpose. Applying this understanding to personal and public affairs would help reset our micro-interpersonal and macro-organizational lives for dynamic leadership that benefits everyone.

Remarkably, when we look at the Constitution's Preamble, we can see how there is a parallel with DNA, whether individual or organizational. The Driver is "We the people of the United States, in Order to form a more perfect union." It is the mission statement. It directs leadership to work for all of America in order to produce a more unified, better America. The Nucleus is to "establish Justice, insure domestic Tranquility, provide for the common defence, and promote the general Welfare." This is a statement of strategy. It sets forth a specific sequence of actions necessary to realize the mission. The Accelerator completes the sequence—"and secure the Blessings of Liberty to ourselves and our Posterity, do ordain and establish this Constitution for the United States of America." Liberty, posterity, Constitution, and America are the touchstones of the most effective leadership which the Congress, the President, and the Supreme Court should generate in fulfillment of our mission as one people, our grand strategy, and our country's leadership.

The new leadership ethic relates to the common defense in many ways, particularly in the "just war theory" which delineates a set of rules for military combat—waged only after all peaceful options are considered. A just war must be in response to a wrong suffered, such as self defense against foreign attack. A just war must have a higher cause with the possibility of success. The primary objective of the war must be to re-establish peace with justice. Violence in a just war must be proportional to the casualties suffered. The use of force can only be justified if civilians are not harmed except as being the unavoidable victims of a military attack on a strategic target. Therefore, America would not enter into the armed conflict of war without just cause, and after all other actions had been taken to avoid it. This would not strike down the nation's willingness to engage an enemy attack to "secure its blessings of liberty." It would mean that we consider it necessary to prepare for war in a way that would lessen, if not eliminate, the prospect of war itself. To keep the promise America made, we must "provide for the common defence."

CHAPTER 6

PROMOTE THE GENERAL WELFARE

Not all creativity is productive. And not all productivity is creative. The idea is to put them together to stimulate abundance for those who are able and assistance for those who are not. Creativity is the productive force of technological innovation, industrial growth, cultural evolution, and political solutions that can be energized, checked and balanced. This has brought a new order to the world which channels a mainstream of action that "promotes the general welfare."

And this is why $I=am^2$, our ticket to creativity, is fundamentally important. It engages an idea, the general welfare, with its implications—justice, domestic tranquility, and the common defense—to associate them, at the tempo of leadership, to produce the blessings of liberty for each other and our posterity. So, it is beyond important that we understand there is a way for solving our political leadership crisis—that is, $I=am^2$ plugged into the Preamble. There is no political reason that should supersede that, once we get to it.

When we get to it is also a function of our ODNA. How our organization (O) as a nation may drive (D) it to form a nucleus (N) at the center, and accelerate (A) its pace of growth and development is, of course, essential. America does have a DNA. So does every other distinct entity. Our DNA, once we settle on what we should know about it, critically defines us as a nation. It tells us what we value and, therefore, how we are differentiated among other nations.

The new leadership ethic is a reflection of how we exercise our values. It tells others who we are, what we are like, and where we are likely to be going. What does it mean for us to be doing the greatest possible good? For the largest number of our citizens? Over the longest period of time? With the lowest necessary cost? All this, as it goes, defines us to ourselves and to others.

Food and shelter, timely healthcare, affordable schooling, good jobs, recreational opportunities, a sense of well-being and a continuing emphasis on quality improvement for all in every aspect of life, emerges from achieving the call of the general welfare. It is very powerful because a healthy metabolism of the body politic rests upon its genuine strength. And it is not something impossible, because we can reasonably achieve it.

It's not enough for corporate profits to rise, for the economy to improve, and for the stock market to soar. These are good things. But what about the one third of all Americans who are living in or near poverty with minimal working class wages? What about falling middle class incomes? What about the lack of spendable assets that so many Americans do not possess, in case of emergency or urgency? A great mass of consumers fit these circumstances..Their spending is a substantial share of the money which moves the products, creates the jobs, and helps drive the economy. When the system is working, opportunities open, investors step in, capital flow picks up, tax revenues rise, and infrastructure is modernized.

As prosperity spreads, crime and incarceration level off, the degree of education rises, healthcare improves, capabilities increase, creativity and innovation grow, community metabolism strengthens, and hopefulness and confidence become more evident. Better targeted social and economic measurements will identify this.

The general interest is better served as the wealth spreads more widely. Participation in democratic processes increases as the number of eligible voters rises, interest in running for public office intensifies, and both economic and political processes get healthier. Indeed, the whole of society becomes more viable and dynamic.

As society functions more effectively, economies become more productive and the nation becomes more efficient, more unified, and stronger. In general, it is a strategy of productivity that the Preamble calls for in its clauses about justice, tranquility, defense, and welfare. This leads to the possibilities of prosperity. This is the basis of the underlying concern for high-energy productivity in human enterprise. This enables us to consider our primal creativity that taps into the infinite energy of the universe.

The core problem is that too many Americans do not have access to opportunity, protection, and dreams of a better life to come. These many are not only deprived, but also disabled from contributing their creative energies to the greater good. And the greater good is dependent upon the success of these many to contribute their energies to help drive a viable and leading society. This is a deeply damaging corruption of the Preamble's intent and the Constitution's purpose. Many who say they support the Constitution and the rule of law are not.

Society is driven by the growth of economic consumption. Without that a society becomes a failing state. Can America fall from being the most powerful leading nation to being a less powerful failing state? Of course it may. One could argue that it has already begun. For that to be turned around as it can and must be, the American people need to demand that political leadership engages their priorities with the intentions of the Preamble in a very public way to engage the public in the beginnings of a lasting debate about how to provide for the future. And today is the beginning of that future.

To keep the promise America made, we must "promote the general Welfare." It underlies the prospect of our future.

PART THREE

OUR LEADERSHIP-THE OUTPUT

CHAPTER 7

SECURE THE BLESSINGS OF LIBERTY

"The truth shall make you free" is a favorite line in scripture and schooling. Creativity is the foundation of freedom. And freedom leads to truth. This is important since the search for truth is so fundamental to the greatest good. Truth and the freedom to pursue it is essential to whatever knowledge is acquired and experienced. And experience is formative for everyone in their relationships.

The Preamble, as the founders saw it, expressed the soul of America's freedom. It sets forth three main conditions:

1) a mission based on the consent of the people as a whole and especially those among them who are striving for a more perfect union;

2) a strategy for establishing justice, insuring domestic tranquility, providing for the common defense and promoting the general welfare, each making way for the next; and

3) a leadership built upon liberty with an eye on the future, founded in a federal constitution and united as a nation of active citizens.

Liberty, or freedom, isn't free. It is held fast by responsibilities. The whole is greater than the sum of its parts. All the parts are interdependent. The mission is the appointed task. The strategy is the joint action. The leadership is the common effort.

America sought its freedom from the oppression of King George III, as Thomas Jefferson wrote in the Declaration of Independence. The Founding Fathers decided then that, as a new nation, they wanted to have freedom to pursue faith, thought and expression. This was subsequently guaranteed in the First Amendment of the new Constitution— and later extended to all of government by the equal protection clause of the Fourteenth

Amendment. First, it was securing freedom from the abusive power of another nation so that second, we could enjoy freedom to pursue the opportunities of our own nation.

The freedom won, however, was accompanied by slavery. And the vestiges of that compromise can be seen in the poverty which still clouds the land. The struggle for progress along the way has been difficult and yet productive. The tenacious leadership of determined advocates has made a big difference. Today, the indomitable freedom quest launched and sparked in the late eighteenth century still faces a polarized American populace in the early twenty-first.

Now, the emergence of terrorism threatens the creative and civilizing potential of human freedom. The interdependence of all peoples is becoming increasingly complex. The priest and paleontologist Teilhard de Chardin observed that "Everything happening in the universe is the result of the success or failure of a primordial urge, which is present in all matter and energy, to combine into structures of increased complexity and consciousness."[23] Humanity.

The more complex and conscious that society is, the more a cohesive center of gravity with a collaborating critical mass and a creative tipping point is necessary. A dominating force would risk damaging all that. Freedom, on the other hand, is at low risk of doing so. The point is to "secure the blessings of liberty" for all. Dominance at any level and any sphere is the polar opposite of $I=am^2$. It runs counter to liberty. And liberty is the essence of America as a prosperous democracy.

We must remember that, as a republican democracy, we are a dynamic body politic. Our ODNA is about our freedom, our liberty. As an organization (O), the creative energy of our freedom is driven (D) to form a center of gravity for our democracy then, in turn, a critical mass from a nucleus (N) of creativity that reaches a tipping point of acceleration (A) for justice toward a chain reaction of peace advancing at the speed of their momentum squared. ODNA.

Freedom is the dynamic energy of engaged decision-making. Democracy is the participation of the people engaged. Creativity is the particular energy that engages the body. Justice is the equality of opportunity and protection in being engaged. Peace is the tranquility among all those who are engaged from the grassroots to the elite.

To keep the promise America was made, we must "secure the Blessings of Liberty."

CHAPTER 8

TO OURSELVES AND OUR POSTERITY

"It's all about the future." Our posterity. That's what I used to say to University of Tampa graduates at commencements each year. And it is. Every step we take is one ahead of the present. So, let's plan on how we wish to address it. If you don't like what you think is going to happen, then change your plans accordingly. What do you wish for? How can you get there? What must you do? What, realistically, can you do? Are you thinking about that? Organizing for that? Changing plans as better thoughts come to mind? Do nothing and you are delegating your future to happenings beyond your control. How smart is that?

This is why you should be thinking ahead as well as you can. This is why you should be imagining, even dreaming, as you get to practical thinking.

Einstein said that "imagination is more important than knowledge."[24] The world we live in is dynamic. Creativity is at a premium. America is an experiment in creativity. This doesn't mean so much that all is change, though sometimes it seems so. Rather, it means that everything is of a type, a kind, and a context of its inner realities in flowing change. We must not forget that both continuity and change are part of the reality we live with. And all of it is how we actually see it. What we are aware of and whatever we are not.

Remember, again, what Professor Brian Greene said in writing about Einstein's discovery: **"There is nothing you can do, not a move you can make, not a thought you can have, that doesn't tap directly into $E=mc^2$. Einstein's equation is constantly at work, providing an unseen hand that shapes the world into its familiar form."** Adam Smith said that moral sentiments are the other side of practical pursuits. What are your moral sentiments? Whatever they are, they will be reflected in your $I=am^2$ profile.

When we think of ourselves in relation to a group, we are always going to find ourselves somewhere in a circle of gravity around a political center. This can plainly be seen by dropping a pebble in a pond and watching the ripples of water flow to the shores around it. $I=am^2$ calls us to the center, where one disturbance can lead to many.

Today is the future, according to $I=am^2$. The future is in our planning, however it is developing now. The plan is always changing, a little or a lot, along with circumstances. Change involves interpretation, how we think about it. Interpretation rises for everyone differently, depending upon perspective. Everyone has a view of the future from wherever they are thinking. And the future is different, at least somewhat, depending upon these thoughts. This is the context from which our leadership emerges, and to which it must be addressed.

Confirmation of Einstein's theory of gravity waves throughout the universe was the "Science Story of

2016."[25] This was exactly one hundred years after he predicted them. The effect of this confirmation is the understanding that the source, or center, of our attractions has a great deal to do with the beliefs, thoughts and actions that comprise our gravitas. And, of course, to help with understanding where we are going, we must understand where our beliefs, thoughts and actions are coming from. This understanding is critical as we try to assess the impact of what we are collectively doing and how long we hope it may last. $I=am^2$, together with ODNA and the new leadership ethic, helps us do that.

Though Washington on *mass,* Franklin on *light,* and Hamilton on *energy,* did not have a formula in mind, what they did have in mind was an eye on the future. That is why the phrase *"to ourselves and our Posterity"* fits persuasively after the phrase about securing the blessings of liberty. The founders' intent was that lawmakers should be looking well down the road as they plan new legislation. And the agendas that special interests had in their time were a serious problem as they are today.

In any organization, clarity of mission must come before any actionable forward movement. This is necessary in order to understand the need for manpower, materials and money. Mission creep—straying from a given charge—is a common trait of faltering organizations. The United States of America is a sovereign government. All governments are a form of organization. They all are established for a purpose and led, at any given time, by a specific mission. With a compelling mission, there will be fewer discrepancies between effectiveness—doing things well—and economy—doing things inexpensively—and are less likely to undermine efficiency—by doing things productively. This was true in the new nation of the late 18th century and is true in the early 21st century today. Leadership is lost when a mission is missing.

In between the expectations of mission and the effects of leadership are the strategic actions that connect them. These must be carefully formulated, continuously reviewed, and collaboratively executed. Otherwise, all sorts of unnecessary trouble will follow. It is not easy for anyone or any organization to properly plan, re-evaluate, and produce. But our future as individuals and organizations depend on it in order to succeed. And, today is the future.

To keep the promise America was made, we must assure benefits "to ourselves and our Posterity."

CHAPTER 9

DO ORDAIN AND
ESTABLISH THIS CONSTITUTION

By pursuing a new leadership ethic, we can nurture the inextinguishable attraction of freedom and democracy that pervades the deepest desires of people across the world. This is central to political leadership in America in that the Constitution provides for a federal government, that is, a national government with state governments in a single political system. For America, the Preamble embodies the spirit of a new leadership ethic. It moderates the extremes of autocracy on the one hand and the extremes of libertarianism on the other. It is not a new idea to consider the difference between an ongoing management ethic and a new leadership ethic in any organization as well as the importance of reconciling the two in order to carry forward the priorities of the organization. The ninth phrase of the Preamble affirms that the

Founders *do ordain and establish this Constitution* to be the basis for the framework of law in the nation.

Command and control, as in management, is not the same as collaboration and consent, as in leadership. The first is derived from a warrior culture led by tribal chiefs who were supported by loyal soldiers. The second is derived from a democratic culture by chosen leaders who are followed by respectful partners. Of course, there are all kinds of gradations, mixes and matches between the two. Certainly they will change as the pendulum swings from times of emergency to times of normality. To ordain, in any case, is to unalterably maintain a value over time by established authority.

Time and circumstances change, and with these changes so do peoples' interpretations. The pursuit of meaning for a generally desired future is what is most important. Original statements were written in the spirit of their times and meaningful for people in those current circumstances. Today, there is a deep debate about whether original statements can and should be interpreted in the same way today as they were when they were written. There is no doubt that the spirit of our times relates necessarily to circumstances that may be vastly different from what they were when written. The spirit of the law carries forward over time, and is always interpreted for a desired future. What is the right answer regarding how the third branch of the governing triumvirate set up by the founders—the judiciary—should interpret those original statements for the future of our nation?

A new leadership ethic has begun to emerge as change comes quicker and as people need to be smarter. It depends in part on making the choice of which value has priority. Is it the value placed on profit first—money, power or fame—or service first—customers, clients or constituents? There is no question they are two sides of the same coin. The priority selected depends on which is the end and which is the means. Fame and fortune or influence and respect? As our current definition of a free country winds, zigzags or loops its way into the future, we face both danger and opportunity. Will we have crisis management or creative leadership or both, and when?

The new leadership ethic has four elements:
1) doing the greatest possible good;
2) for the largest number of people;
3) over the longest period of time;
4) at the lowest necessary cost.

This matches up with our leading equation—impetus, action, and momentum—plus the Preamble's formulation of mission, strategy and leadership—to create what we believe to be the empowering $I=am^2$ code of purpose which frames a system of leadership that can be measured.

These then combine effectiveness and economy for the sake of optimum efficiency and productivity. Prosperity then results from successful application. Can we imagine that our impetus is the greatest good, that our actions are for the largest number of people, that our momentum is to be sustained for the longest period of time, and that its multiplier effect enables the most productive possible outcome given the circumstances.

Order begins with adherence to the law of the land embodied in the Constitution, from its first sentence in the Preamble to its last in the 27th Amendment. Our political leaders are sworn to take the Constitution seriously. Members of Congress, the President, and the Justices of the Supreme Court take an oath of office to support and defend it. The Founding Fathers created the Constitution in that frame of mind.

To keep the promise America made, we must see to it that, in fact, we do ordain and establish this Constitution.

CHAPTER 10

FOR THE UNITED STATES OF AMERICA

As we return to the promise America was made by our founders to "We the People" and to the moral suasion of their leadership, it seems to be only appropriate to imagine how the arc of the universe is on the side of liberty and justice "for the United States of America." This is the final phrase of the Preamble. It is meant for America, yet it also is relevant for all beyond our shores, near and far, who are responsive in their own ways to the universality of the American idea and its influence.

In the $I=am^2$ ("we are") equation, the squared symbol is the force multiplier which is multiplied by itself to produce a result which, in this case, is momentum. A force multiplier is a term that, when applied to military troops, refers to an attribute that dramatically increases their fighting effectiveness, giving them the ability to accomplish much more than what they would have otherwise been able to do. This attribute generates a wave of emotion with a pronounced speed of thought. They engage the force multiplier on a mission of importance that will enable achieving a higher level of unity in an aspiring group. How will this happen? How does enthusiasm burst into riveted attention, thoughtful concentration and sustained dedication?

We go back to $I=am^2$ as our leading equation to build an *impetus* of leadership that is equal to the task of converting the *actions* of individual people into the *momentum* of the whole population, unified in response to that impetus. This equation of leadership then sends a stirring signal, with a compelling message, that rapidly resonates among participants. Its gravitational pull would then be so pronounced that the attraction would be instantaneous and ongoing. It would lead to a boost in morale and a supercharge of energy in the group. The civic rock would be on a dynamic roll, the soul of freedom would be aroused and the empowerment of all would take charge. This would be the spirit of America.

History teaches that achieving these goals is difficult and so is not often achieved because it takes such patience and diligence. To do all this would require mastering the most creative information, the most collaborative participation, the most visionary cause, the most concerted strategy, and the most connecting resources possible, given time and circumstance, with the efforts involved in pulling it all together, and then taking its measure.

The cause of America is in the Constitution's Preamble of freedom and leadership. The door of freedom is left open for all Americans, now including women, African and Asian Americans, Latinos, and many others. It applies to people everywhere. It is, arguably, the momentum of the world. $I=am^2$ is, in effect, the algorithm of a human force multiplier in which "we are" in a land of freedom and democracy. Any dominating force, sooner or later, is its opposite: a force detractor.

To keep the promise America made, it must be for "the United States of America."

PART FOUR

THE MORAL QUIVALENT OF WAR

CHAPTER 11

A NEW ACCOUNTABILITY

It's not true, as many believe, that we can't do anything about our compromised political system now. Yes, we can if we frame a solution as "the moral equivalent of war." Most people don't want war. At this moment, we are not acting so much as law keepers of the public interest as we are law breakers for our personal interests. This may be in our nature, of course, but we do need a better balance of the two if our most powerful nation is going to thrive as a free country into the future. Therefore, the conscience of America must be at our center of gravity in restoring the national conversation. To ignore this demand and opportunity would violate the spirit, if not the letter, of the law. This is a slippery slope, and is precisely where the Preamble comes in.

Legal interpretations of the law vary, so it is important to understand the circumstances underlying the concept that launched the basic document of this new nation. We were given a menu that those preparing the recipes over time could follow to give nourishment for this most special nation.

Creativity has always been at the heart of America's leadership. Destruction, though, has subverted that. Look, for example, at how the world turned toward us after the shock of the 9-11 disaster. And then remember how that changed in its aftermath when we chose to attack Afghanistan instead of grasping the opportunity to rally world sympathy into collaborative action and substantive difference. What followed was one problem building to another until our confidence plunged seven years later as the stock market crashed, the Great Recession struck home, and millions of Americans were its victims.

The U.S. Constitution's Preamble is the national purpose of the United States and the foundation on which America's democracy is interpreted. The mission, strategy and leadership of the nation are empowered by its narrative. It frames the articles and amendments that follow it. Now, circumstances necessitate a different public conversation about a more encouraging future in America and the world.

America urgently needs a new accounting of the national condition that leads from the first principles of the Preamble to the financial consequences of our annual budgets. Embedded in the first sentence of the U.S. Constitution are the creative energies that secure the freedom of the nation and produce a critical mass that sustains a reaction of ongoing support. In the digital world of today, moving at light speed through our electronic universe, everything is affected, from "the common defence" to the "general Welfare", and ultimately the conscience of the country.

This first sentence of the Constitution—its Preamble—presents the standards by which we can be called to account as a nation. Our means of doing that must involve the best information available, with the broadest scope and the most astute analysis. The founders created this Constitution to launch a new governing process that has been, imperfectly but insistently over the years, the basis for success of these United States and a model for nations around the world.

In the clauses of the Preamble, there are ten standards of performance which constitute the national purpose of the United States:

We the People of the United States, in Order to form a more perfect Union, establish Justice, insure domestic Tranquility, provide for the common defence, promote the general Welfare, and secure the Blessings of Liberty to ourselves and our Posterity, do ordain and establish this Constitution for the United States of America.

These are the national ideals against which the condition of America should be considered. Altogether they are the rationale of the nation including why we exist, for whom we exist, what we want to accomplish, how we are intending to do that, and where our resources will come from.

Each of these ten standards must be examined annually and represented as broadly significant performance indicators of American life. Each would be networked with the others to produce one comprehensive analysis of American realities related to the founding ideals of the Preamble. They would be announced as a set of metrics, each one describing a qualitative measure of impact for discussion by the public, the press, and officials in all sectors of society. These discussions would be organized to lead modifications of law, regulation and policy that respond to the findings and the circumstances which accompany them.

Such a new accounting map of the national condition would ask whether those involved with the governing of America are making good on the promise of the founders in the Preamble. How empowered, how free, how capable are Americans in regard to the standards of the Preamble? What is their state of well-being? Here are some leading questions:

1)*"**We the People of the United States**"*: Are we, as a free people, well educated, able and willing voters for their own political leaders at all levels of government? Are we, each of us equally and all of us collectively, fully enfranchised to determine who holds elective office? Our first metric would focus on ***well-informed voting***.

2)*"**in Order to form a more perfect Union**"*: Are we able to function efficiently in the halls of government as a whole leadership body in our common cause? Is this our land, one people working together with respect for the law of the land? Our second metric would assess ***effective government.***

3) *"establish Justice"*: Do we live in a fair land where everyone is receiving equal treatment by and before the law in all sectors and at every level of society? Our third metric would examine the presence of **equal justice under law**.

4) *"insure domestic Tranquility"*: Is ours a peaceful land with responsible public servants of the people, by the people, for the people, and accountable to the people? Our fourth metric would ascertain the status of **public service**.

5) *"provide for the common defence"*: Are we in a safe land that protects against foreign attack by threats of any type from any source anywhere? Our fifth metric would determine the status of our **mutual security**.

6) *"promote the general Welfare"*: Are we the promised land of opportunity and solidarity that is necessary for common prosperity. Our sixth metric of opportunities would consider the **well-being of citizens**.

7) ***"and secure Blessings of Liberty"***: Do we live in the land of the free in which all people. as the Declaration of Independence says "are endowed by their Creator with certain inalienable Rights, that among these are Life, Liberty and the pursuit of Happiness?" The seventh metric would analyze the presence of ***freedom amid diversity***.

8) ***"to ourselves and our Posterity"***: Are we the home of the brave, where people are confident of better lives in a prosperous and sustainable future? The eighth metric would calculate the cost benefits of ***optimum productivity***.

9) ***"do ordain and establish this Constitution"***: How well does our fundamental dependence on law and order prevent disorder in its legislative, executive, and judicial branches? The ninth metric would value the status of ***law enforcement*** from the top down.

10) *"for the United States of America"*: Is our leadership in the free world integral to the nation's pursuit of freedom in domestic as well as foreign affairs? This tenth and prime metric would evaluate the primary facets of *America's leadership* in the world.

The ten standards are integral parts of a body politic whose current condition will reflect, in essence, the promises of the U.S. Constitution in general and its Preamble in particular. To do that urgently and effectively mandates an annual assessment available to the public.

Because it is essential to measure how well the promises in the new Constitution of 1787 are being realized, a new instrument is necessary to compare how well the spirit of the law is alive in the country. We will need to have an annual set of promise markers based on the standards outlined above, organized according to our $I{=}am^2$ code of purpose, using the latest data and analysis. Performance measures will best serve political leaders in an objective and nonpartisan way. As Americans become better informed by such analyses, American government would become more effective, more economical and ultimately more efficient. This would strengthen the nation as a whole and enable it to regain its stature as the standard for freedom, productivity and leadership across the world.

CHAPTER 12
KEEPING THE PROMISE

As the leading dynamic that wires together America's higher purpose, $I=am^2$ understood simply as "we are," is the framework for keeping the promise America was made by its Founding Fathers. It is the gatekeeper and the guide star for leadership in any chosen direction. How may we best take advantage of the opportunity it offers? The problem is one of priorities.

To start with, it is difficult to think about how a political leader can swear to God to support and defend the Constitution, then explicitly disregard its foundation of our ideals for freedom and democracy as set forth in the Preamble. It is less difficult to imagine that political and personal interests have become more important than the national interest.

As Bret Stephens cautioned about failed peace agreements: "Abandon all principle, ye who enter here," a sign that could be, regardless of party, posted over the West Wing door of the White House and, for that matter, in the halls of Congress and the Supreme Court as well.[26] But easy pragmatism does not negate hard principle, it simply shrinks it from greater purpose to lesser purpose, for example, from the people to a person. That is why the national purpose is so significant. Who are we really helping?

At home and abroad, therefore, political leadership is our greatest challenge, especially now that disunity threatens peace and good will in our nation and the world in which America's global leadership has been most notable for three quarters of a century.

The nature of leadership is framed by the $I=am^2$ dynamic of high purpose as it is plugged into the issues of everyday people in an objective and nonpartisan way. To help us pursue that, we must identify the patterns these issues take as they rise and fall.

There are three major sets of issues that, because of the realities of daily living and the daily news coverage in one form or another, have most to do with the living conditions to which everyone is or should be paying attention: economic growth, mutual security, and national governability. These issues, of course, affect people differently. The greater and more accurate the awareness we have about them as they affect us, the better off we all are going to be. Unhappy people can create expensive problems. Happy people can help solve them.

So we'll check out the key people who aspire to represent us as public servants. We'll have a better understanding of why we trust them, or of whatever risks there may be in giving them our trust. Are we reasonably certain of their values that we are relying on? We often are not giving much thought about why we are leaning one way or another in voting. Self-centeredness is not necessarily a good thing, especially if it is attached primarily to personal gain. If enough of us make poor choices, it will endanger our lives in America and our influence in the world. Remember $I=am^2$, that "we are."

Economic growth is the impetus of our national purpose, the creative energy of its leading equation, and the driver of its dynamics. It sparks the energy of the human spirit and the source of good jobs. It generates the creative force of the world as we know it. The Gross Domestic Product or GDP is the most often used measure of economic growth today, but it does not actually measure a number of the impacts that affect people who are, therefore, not seen in its data. The devil is in the details. And the details require more astute measurements, such as we are planning in the Promise America Reports.

Therefore, we pay attention to the first two clauses of the Preamble which everybody knows—"We the People of the United States, in Order to form a more perfect Union"—and forget the rest of the ten clauses which we presumably learned in school and which supply definition to the national purpose.

Economic growth enhances greater productivity in a potentially healthier and stronger civic society. Productive capacity is a function of working capital, high technology, hard work, and adequate literacy in the presence of a decent and sustainable environment. Productivity alone, without sustainability, is eventually nonproductive. People fall by the wayside and need enforcement, some degree of public support they otherwise wouldn't need. Growth goes down and taxes go up. Altogether unsustainable.

Mutual security is all about the actions of leading individuals and powerful organizations that, together, develop a measurable critical mass which evolves into an atmosphere of public safety—both the nation's military and our state and local policing—as the common cause. This is accomplished through projections and protections of political and economic power, direct diplomacy, law enforcement and military might.

Critical mass involves unification and unification is essential for power. Power requires people to pay attention and take action together for a shared purpose they feel strongly about. Critical mass translates into political power that can burst through a tipping point into a chain reaction that is sustainable so long as people support it.

Unification is a development of common cause. Holding that together requires the Preamble's conditions of justice, tranquility, defense, and welfare. They, in sequence, are the makings of a grand strategy for America that leads directly to the makings of liberty not only for ourselves, but for future generations. While the Founding Fathers did not mention a grand strategy, that is what they effectively created in the Preamble.

National governability is about the momentum of political leadership of the highest order. This requires a Congress, a President, and a Supreme Court working not only as three independent branches of government, but also as interdependent branches of one government. This will critically involve broad agreement on the Preamble's principles because each branch has different functions and practices. If there is common cause centered on the Preamble as the heart of American leadership, there will be a greater likelihood of governability and a lesser likelihood of dysfunction. This is true for all levels and sectors of our free and democratic society each of which is measurable.

Take the U.S. Marine Corps as an example. It is built on the idea of "duty, honor, and country." It is well known for its strength and effectiveness. A marine dedicates his or her individuality to the greater power of mission, strategy, and leadership to get a mission accomplished without any distractions or influences from other sources. Therefore, duty begins with the mission. Honor is the product of enacting a strategy. Country is the high purpose of its leadership. The mission is the impetus. The strategy enables the action. The leadership engages the momentum. $I=am^2$ is the translator of high purpose and the driver of leadership.

National governability would, ideally, never be an issue. But, of course, it constantly is. Precisely because there is no shared vision of purpose and no inherent idea of how to work for that. Enter $I=am^2$ as the core dynamic of purpose. This powerful dynamic calls for a common understanding of the mission that is strong enough to catch and guide the attention of the leading participants. It then calls for a concerted strategy that is clear enough to advance the intended mission. And, finally, it calls for ongoing leadership to develop momentum and carry on for as long as necessary.

With new eyes, then, there is greater clarity of mission, strategy, and leadership emerging and their momentum growing. $I=am^2$ helps us plan and promote the most important steps forward and to do so methodically. We can watch the news and more likely perceive what reality is unfolding and what adjustments must be made to address it. $I=am^2$ is a constant support to keep up with events as they arise.

Economic growth, mutual security, and national governability become the organizers of thoughts and action. Keeping the promise that has been made to Americans becomes more doable if people are keeping pace with changing circumstances. And that's what governments are for—to do for us what we cannot do for ourselves in order to improve the lives of our citizens, as Abraham Lincoln so importantly observed.

The American DNA—freedom, with democracy and creativity, justice and peace—is born and raised according to these foundations. What is true for the DNA of individual citizens is also true for the ODNA of individual organizations. Organizational DNA is analogous to the seed from which the future germinates. The ODNA contains our genetic code. The ODNA lifestream is the equivalent of an individual cell's protoplasm which is, we might say, the superfluid leading to the growth of organisms, whether singular as with persons or complex as with organizations.

The $I=am^2$ code of purpose includes the ODNA as the equivalent of being the Driver, Nucleus, and Acceleration of an organization as a moving body which Einstein called "The Electrodynamics of Moving Bodies." The ODNA's dynamic sequence may evolve in quantum leaps of maturation. It does so as an integrated circuit with instructions of memory stored on a molecular leader chip flowing from the heart to the brain for guiding the organization of its transforming leadership.

In an organization, as Bill Gates has seen it, "a digital nervous system is the corporate digital equivalent of the human nervous system."[27] As he saw it, information technology is the only way to have sufficiently quick reflexes for connecting business strategy and organizational response.

Governing the leadership required to run such organizations, and especially such nations, it is important to know that they are not machines. They are led and managed by human beings. The rules which frame them are derived from the principles which encode their ODNAs. How these principles are interpreted are, then, the responsibility of the organization's leaders at all levels and in all spheres of its role and scope.

$I=am^2$ is engraved on the leader chip of high purpose. Purpose is our highest and most significant underlying principle. It transcends all legal issues related to the rule of law. It entails human responsibility at its core. If we face a "jungle of legal peril" as Philip Howard put it, the role of purpose should be understood as engaging the moral suasion that would undo it. Law can't think, but people can. They can see rules related to the principles they presumably uphold and ask themselves if they comport with the highest of American values, which are found in the Preamble. If there is a standard model of civics, it would be $I=am^2$, the moral equivalent of war.

CHAPTER 13
LEADER OF THE FREE WORLD

"The United States does not rule or govern, as much as it leads from the power of its model," as Jeremi Suri observes. The global community functions by organizational "cooperation on American terms" and assesses America's competitiveness in foreign trade and domestic affairs on its own terms.[28]

The U.S. must decide what leadership role it will purposefully commit to serving in the world of the future. On what terms will we collaborate with and compete within the leading alliances of which we are part? In what spheres and levels will we do so?

If the U.S. wishes to recover its role as "leader of the free world," it must be as an exemplar of freedom and democracy as well as a leading competitor in critical technology. That is the leverage of its power in our civilized world.

If the U.S. is to recharge its leadership of the free world, it must balance its equality, its prosperity, and its competitiveness. That is the legitimacy of its creative impact on the world community.

If the U.S. is to renew its leadership of the free world, it must sustain its commitment to justice and the peace. That must be the nature of our leadership to foster credibility around the increasingly globalized world.

The strength of U.S. leadership of the free world, therefore, is always a combination of its present influence on hearts and minds alongside its preset capacity of finance and fight. Our hard power must be at the ready in support. Our soft power must be at the ready and in the lead.

Multilateral U.S. alliances would generally be priority while bilateral relationships would be sought wherever and whenever necessary and proper. The realities of globalized relationships would presumably help overcome the risks of U.S. isolation and confrontation.

The U.S. would be seen as the competitive standard-bearer in the nuances of free trade and the reliable defender of a rule-based order as a proponent of universality and an opponent of protectionism.

U.S. grand strategy in the macro world in which it lives would always take account of the specific tactics in the micro world of which it is composed.

All this leads to the rewiring of U.S. leadership and competitiveness as one amicable nation acting in accordance with the dynamics of a global system of many different and competitive nations.

None of such rewiring would threaten the greater interests of the American people. Instead, it would intentionally lead to their greater good.

That is because the greatest possible good, for the largest number of people, over the longest period of time, at the lowest necessary cost would become the architecture of a new leadership ethic. This would replace the old management practices which may, if continuously dominant, threaten us today.

This is why the conduct of leaders who set the agenda for action is so important. What is the meaning of what they say and do? Who would benefit from that and who would not? Are they worthy of our trust? In the end that trust is essential.

And this is why the Preamble of our Constitution is so central to our thinking about America's future. It frames the issues of political debate. It is interpreted for the tomorrows of everyone. It underlies the strength of our national capabilities and our global competitiveness.

The Preamble is the baseline of all political measures because it is the introduction to our Constitution and, therefore, to the rule of law. It has broadly stated support in the country, but only narrowly actual support in the realms of public policy and political action, and is virtually a dead letter in legal precedent.

Using the $I=am^2$ model, we can dissect the sequence of the Preamble's wording to better fathom the framers' intent. The mission of America, its impetus, is captured in the way the Preamble opens: "We the People of the United States, in Order to form a more perfect Union."

The strategy of America, the action it takes, follows in the subsequent words: "establish Justice, insure domestic Tranquility, provide for the common defence, promote the general Welfare".

The leadership of America, its momentum, is summed up in its closing words: "secure the Blessings of Liberty to ourselves and our Posterity, do ordain and establish this Constitution for the United States of America".

As a politically organized system, the U.S. has is own identity, or ODNA, to which the rewiring of $I=am2$ is connected. The organization (O) speaks to America as a nation. The driver (D) is the People who are leading the more perfect Union. The nucleus (N)—Justice, Tranquility, defence, Welfare—powers up the national engine. The accelerator (A)—Liberty, Posterity,

Constitution, America—picks up and sustains the national momentum.

The new leadership ethic develops, from the ODNA body politic, the greatest possible good for the entire organized system. It reaches the largest number of citizens it can within that system. It stretches over the longest period of time it is able to. And it does so with the fewest necessary resources.

From this progression arises the American ideology—that is, its foundation of core values—which guides the body politic and produces the American culture in all its diversity and features. As this is reflected in our culture, we may define ourselves as the leader of the free world, with all our blemishes, the greatest country in history.

There is, though, one unavoidable condition for being so defined. The dynamics of our body politic must be sustained by the high purpose of the Preamble—the moral equivalent of war, as the founders clearly intended—at the interminable speed of $I=am^2$ creativity, as the founders surely assumed.

AFTERWORD

American citizens' quality of life and well-being, and that of their guests, comes before every other consideration, whether legal or financial, political or moral. The individual dignity of each person is absolute, regardless of who they are or what they are doing. Respect for each and every one is non-negotiable according to the declaration of "equal justice under law" as the Supreme Court publicly headlines atop its entryway in Washington.

This leads to an apparent paradox between respect for individual dignity and regard for economic growth. The first is the end and the second is the means. Economic growth opens the door to greater opportunities and thus to greater respect for individual possibilities. But the means must not become the end or wealth supplants health and societies die. The relationship between the two is interdependent and coexistent.

That we must monetize in order to civilize the world order is not a contradiction. To monetize is to create a medium of exchange which facilitates trade between and among cooperating parties. This advances investment and the capitalization of assets which, in turn, leads to wealth creation. So long as the dignity of the individual—any person—is not harmed or subjugated in the process, it leads to improvement of the whole—whether a family, a village, or the nation of which that person is a part. When harm is done, it devalues not only the individual, but also the human connections of which an individual is part.

As David Pilling has notably observed in *The Growth Delusion*[22], we are in an "age of anger" that has produced a "popular backlash." This is the outcome of a grossly widening gap in income and assets of the wealthiest Americans vis-a-vis all the others. Those living in poverty and near poverty have grown to one-third of the American population. In the meantime, the middle class has shrunk to less than half the population. Many Americans are frustrated by the polarized political process and the failure of Washington to get its act together.

American leadership is not coexistent with economic productivity by itself, but it is coexistent with human productivity in general. Leadership is about what people do. How they invest their economic assets is part of that. Financial productivity is an outcome of what leadership does or does not do. It is very much a condition of human productivity. Human capital generates financial capital which together sustain the momentum of leadership.

The Gross Domestic Product or GDP of a nation is a valuable economic indicator that measures the monetary value of select goods and services produced in a given period of time, commonly on an annual basis. It does not measure the quality of life or well-being of the people of a nation. What we are searching for is an indicator that will measure the changes in living conditions that the American people do or do not enjoy as these conditions may be inferred from the promise America was made in the Preamble of the U.S. Constitution, and these promises should be understood as "positive commands to government to perform its duties in the best interest of the people," as the legal historian Peter Charles Hoffer has observed. [29]

An annual Promise America Report, or PAR, as mentioned, will be structured to address a new accounting of the Constitution's leadership in American life. It will assess how well "We the People of the United States, in

Order to form a more perfect Union" is working as the authority and **mission** of the country. It will then assess how well "establish Justice, insure domestic Tranquility, provide for the common defence, promote the general Welfare" is working as the **strategy** of the country to carry forward its mission. And finally, it will assess how well we approach our **leadership** "and secure the Blessings of Liberty to ourselves and our Posterity, do ordain and establish this Constitution for the United States of America" is working to shape the future of the country.

In order for the best made plans to thrive, there must be a new accountability for Americans. That accounting must have the conscience of the country at its center of gravity. The American spirit would be continuously renewed from that creative energy out of which would build a succession of critical mass evolutions that convert to an ongoing momentum of leadership.

But this momentum must arise from its roots in the Preamble to grow fulsomely into a strong standing tree of life for all that would seek the sustenance of its shadow and shade. The energy of the spirit, as the great American physicist and philosopher David Bohm put it:

is conveyed in the word spirit whose root meaning is 'wind, or breath.' This suggests an invisible but pervasive energy to which the manifest world of the finite belongs. This energy, or spirit, infused all living beings, and without it any organism must fall apart into its constituent elements. That which is truly alive in the living being is this energy of spirit, and this is never born and never dies.[30]

The Preamble of the US Constitution is the single foundation of the American spirit. For all the useful knowledge regarding the nation's economy that GDP provides, it does not pointedly serve the national purpose of the

United States. The PAR, our envisioned Promise America Report, intends –year-by-year– to fill the gap.

GDP is the best known and most frequently used measure of macro-economic activity and the standard measure of how well America and other nations around the world presumably are doing. It has become the benchmark used by policy makers throughout the world to debate and reach decisions. GDP aggregates the value-added of selected money-based activities. It is, arguably, too important to be left in the hands of economists alone. It is a pursuit of the social sciences in general, including scholars and practitioners engaged with such information that affects current and future generations, including the destiny of the planet itself.

There are two major challenges in moving beyond GDP toward a comprehensive indicator of human well-being as PAR intends to be. One is economic and relates to how well we address the productivity of goods and services. The other is social and involves how best to obtain reliable information on peoples' prosperity, and particularly their quality of life. The primary emphasis of PAR will be to measure contemporary impacts on "the pursuit of happiness", as Thomas Jefferson famously used the term in the Declaration of Independence.

The need to improve data and other indicators to complement GDP is being increasingly recognized and currently the focus of a number of domestic and international initiatives that reflect updated demographic priorities. The overall aim is to develop more comprehensive and coherent indicators that provide a more reliable knowledge base for public debate and policy-making as in the PAR, which would be the only one derived from the Preamble.

Citizens commonly feel distanced from statistical information and more so if they don't see how it affects them. Basing the PAR in the mission, strategy, and leadership of the Constitution's Preamble would presumably have the overwhelming support of the American people. Citizens care fundamentally about their quality of life. Information and analysis of their prosperity—including their health, their day-to-day necessities, and their opportunities to get ahead—would potentially have great impact on their thinking and their engagement with the political process.

The promises of the Preamble come down to indicating that economic and social cohesion is an overarching intention of the Founding Fathers. Their aim was to reduce harmful disparities and imminent threats to the future of the people. That begins with the Preamble.

NOTES:

1. www.constitution.org/wj.meow.htm

2. www.quotewise,com/bill-gatesquotes-21.html

3. www.alberteinstein.com/quote/einsteinsquotes.html

4. Hawking, Steven & Mindinow, Leonard. *The Grand Design* (2010). Bantam Books, New York.

5. Lederman, Leon & Hill, Christopher. *Beyond the God Particle (2013).* Prometheus Books, Amherst, New York.

6. www.az quotes.com/quote/605857

7. https://www.youtube.com/watch?v=yevITdMsY61

8.Calber, Nigel. *Einsten's Universe.* (1979). Wings Books. New York, N.Y. P. 13.

9. https://www.goalcast.com/2018/04/09/11-margaret-mead-quotes/

10. Tutu, Desmond. *Believe: The Words and Inspiration of Desmond Tutu.* (2007). P.Q. Blackwell, Ltd. Ashland, New Zealand. P. 4.

11. Declaration of Independence (1776)

12. www.abrahamlincoln.org/speeches/liberty.htm.

13.
http://www.sacred-texts.com/aor/einstein/einsci.htm

14.
www.nytimes.com/2005/04/08/opinion/onehundredy
earsofuncertainty.html.

15. Ferris, Timothy. *The Science of Liberty: Democracy, Reason and the Laws of Nature,* (2010) Harper Collins, New York, NY.

16. Wood, Gordon B. *The Idea of America: Reflections on the Birth of the United States.* (2011). Harper Collins, New York, N.Y.

17.
https://history.hanover.edu/courses/excerpts/111feder
alist.html

18.
www.mountvernon.org/library/digitalhistory/quotes/a
rticle/to-be-prepared-for-war-is-one-of-the-most-
effective-means-of -preserving-peace.

19.   https://aboutleaders.com/leaders-honor-thy-
people/

20.   https://www.history.com/speeches/franklin-d-
roosevelts-first-inaugural-address

21.
http://forum.objectivismonline.com/index.php?/topic/

20968-william-jamess-moral-equivalent-of-war-essay/

22.	http://wjmi.blogspot.com/2010/05/liberty-requires-unity_03.html

23. Teilhard de Chardin, Pierre. *The Phenomenon of Man.* (2015). The Great Library Collection by R.P. Pryne.

24. www.gurteen.com/gurteen/gurteen.nsf/id/X0002880 A/

25.	www.nytimes.com/2016/02/12/science/ligo-gravitational-waves-black-holes-einstein-html

26.	www.Afr.com/opinion/columnists/the-us-is-being-played-by-pyongyang-again-20180429-hOzeez

27. https://books.google.com/border?id=AF84fBmnzmV YC&pg=PA367&lpg=PA367&dq=Bill+Gates+quote +A+digital+nervous+system+is+the+corporate+equiv alent+of+the+human+nervous+system.

28. Suri, Jerimi. *Liberties' Surest Guardian (2011). Free Press. P. 33*

29. Pilling, David. *The Great Delusion: Wealth, Poverty and the Well-Being of Nations.* (2018) Tim Duggan Books, New York.

30. Hoffer, Peter Charles. *For Ourselves and Our Posterity: The Preamble to the Federal Constitution in American History.* (2012) Oxford University Press, NY.

31. Peat, F. David. *Infinite Potential: The Life and Times of David Bohm.* (1997) Aedison-Wesly, Reading, MA. P. 22.

Dick Cheshire is Chairman of the Promise America Alliance, author of *Leading by Heart* which proposes a new model of civic leadership in America, and *The Indomitable Freedom Quest* which discusses the Preamble of the Constitution as the centerpiece of American leadership.

He served as president of The University of Tampa and of the New Jersey Shakespeare Festival, as Executive Director of the Shakespeare Globe Centre of North America, vice president and chief development officer of the Center for Strategic & International Studies, Chapman University, Colgate University, and Drew University, a visiting scholar at New York University, and professor of organizational leadership at Chapman.

He has been a teacher and scholar as well as a practitioner and administrator of leadership over his working lifetime. He has an A.B. degree from Colgate

University., an Ed.M. from the University. of New Hampshire, and a Ph.D. from New York University.

He and his wife Bobbie live in Hamilton, New York.